South Carolina

by the Capstone Press
Geography Department

Reading Consultant:
Willie Harriford
South Carolina Department of Education

CAPSTONE PRESS
MANKATO, MINNESOTA

C A P S T O N E   P R E S S

818 North Willow Street • Mankato, Minnesota 56001

Library of Congress Cataloging-in-Publication Data
South Carolina/by the Capstone Press Geography Department
p. cm.--(One Nation)
Includes bibliographical references and index.
Summary: Gives an overview of the state of South Carolina, including its history, geography, people, and living conditions.
ISBN 1-56065-502-X
1. South Carolina--Juvenile literature. [1. South Carolina.]
I. Capstone Press. Geography Dept. II. Series.
F269.3.S68 1997
975.7--dc20

96-35114
CIP
AC

Photo credits
Root Resources/James Blank, cover; MacDonald, 8, 21
Flag Research Center, 4 (left)
Daybreak/Todd Fink, 4 (right)
Unicorn/Dick Keen, 5 (left); Andre Jenny, 5 (right)
Visuals Unlimited/Gary Carter, 10; Audrey Gibson, 26
Lynn M. Stone, 12
Lynn Seldon, 16, 18, 34
FPG, 22, 28
William B. Folsom, 25
James P. Rowan, 30, 32

Table of Contents

Fast Facts about South Carolina

State Flag

Location: In the southern United States, along the Atlantic Ocean

Size: 32,008 square miles (83,221 square kilometers)

Population: 3,642,718 (1993 United States Census Bureau figures)

Capital: Columbia

Date admitted to the Union: May 23, 1788; the eighth state

Carolina wren

Yellow jessamine

Largest cities: Columbia, Charleston, North Charleston, Greenville, Spartanburg, Sumter, Rock Hill, Mount Pleasant, Florence, Anderson

Nickname: The Palmetto State

State animal: White-tailed deer

State bird: Carolina wren

State flower: Yellow jessamine

State tree: Palmetto

State song: "Carolina" by Henry Timrod and Anne Curtis Burgess

Palmetto

Chapter 1

Darlington Raceway

Thousands of racing fans celebrate Labor Day weekend in Darlington, South Carolina. They fill this small town every year. They come to see the Mountain Dew Southern 500 at Darlington Raceway. This stock car race is called the "Granddaddy of Them All."

Darlington Raceway is one of the nation's oldest major speedways. The NMPA Stock Car Hall of Fame is there.

The Joe Weatherly Museum is also at the raceway. It has the world's largest collection of stock cars. Visitors can see many winning cars.

Thousands of racing fans come to Darlington Raceway to see stock car racing.

Some were driven by such famous drivers as Richard Petty and Fireball Roberts.

The Palmetto State

South Carolina's nickname is the Palmetto State. The palmetto is the state tree. In 1776, South Carolinians built a fort with palmetto logs. They called it Fort Moultrie. It was on Sullivans Island and guarded Charleston Harbor during the Revolutionary War (1775-1783).

British ships fired on Fort Moultrie. The palmetto wood stood up against the British cannonballs. Since then, South Carolinians have honored the palmetto.

Something for Everyone

South Carolina is the smallest state in the South. Still, it offers South Carolinians and visitors many activities.

Charleston has beautiful old homes and churches. Swimmers and boaters enjoy the sandy beaches along the Atlantic Coast. Campers use South Carolina's many state parks and forests. Hikers walk along Blue Ridge Mountain trails.

Charleston is known for its beautiful old houses.

Chapter 2
The Land

South Carolina is a southern state. Two other southern states are its neighbors. North Carolina lies to the north. Georgia is to the west and south.

East of South Carolina is the Atlantic Ocean. The state's lowest point is along the coast. That point is sea level.

South Carolinians divide their state into two parts. One part is the Low Country. The other is the Up Country.

The Low Country is a flat, sandy plain. It is near the ocean. To the west and north is the Up Country. Hills rise up to mountains there.

South Carolina is on the Atlantic coast.

Beautiful marshes cover the land along the rivers.

The Atlantic Coastal Plain

Another name for the Low Country is the
Atlantic Coastal Plain. This plain covers two-
thirds of South Carolina. Sandy beaches line
the northern coast. The longest beach is called
the Grand Strand. It is about 60 miles (96
kilometers) long.

Many bays have formed south of the Grand
Strand. The largest bays include Winyah Bay

and Charleston Harbor. South Carolina's rivers flow from the bays into the Atlantic. Major rivers include the Pee Dee, Santee, and Savannah.

Marshes run inland along the rivers. A dam on the Santee River formed Lake Marion. This is South Carolina's largest lake.

Many islands lie off South Carolina's coast. Hilton Head is a resort island. Parris Island has a Marine Corps (KORE) training base.

The Piedmont

The Piedmont covers most of the Up Country. Piedmont means "at the foot of the mountain." The Blue Ridge Mountains rise to the northwest.

The Piedmont has rolling hills. The land is good for farming. South Carolina's rivers run swiftly through the Piedmont. They provide electric power for factories.

At the eastern edge of the Piedmont is the fall line. At the fall line, rivers tumble over a steep ridge to the coastal plain. Columbia is a fall-line city. It lies along the Congaree River.

The Blue Ridge Mountains

The Blue Ridge Mountains form a small part of the Up Country. They are in South Carolina's northwestern corner.

Sassafras Mountain is in the Blue Ridge range. It reaches 3,554 feet (1,066 meters) above sea level. This is the highest point in South Carolina.

Plants and Animals

Almost two-thirds of South Carolina is covered with forests. Spanish moss hangs from oak and cypress trees. Spanish moss is a soft, rubbery plant.

White-tailed deer live in the forests. The marshes are home to black bears and alligators. Wild turkeys and quail are some South Carolina birds. Bass and trout swim in the rivers and lakes.

Climate

South Carolina's Low Country has warm, humid summers. Humid mean the air is heavy with moisture. Strong wind storms called

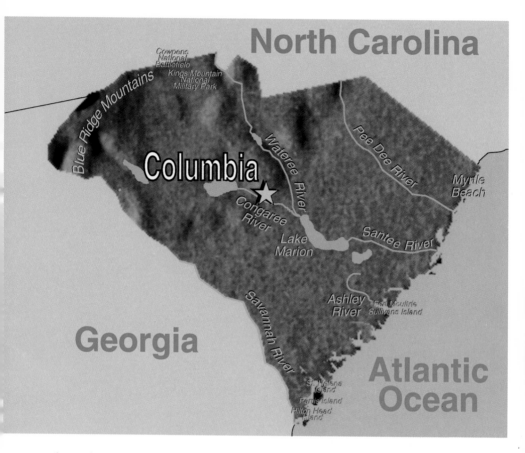

hurricanes sometimes hit the coast. In winter, temperatures average about 50 degrees Fahrenheit (10 degrees Celsius).

The Up Country is cooler in both winter and summer. The Blue Ridge Mountains receive the state's heaviest rainfall. The state does not get much snow. A small amount falls in the mountains.

Chapter 3
The People

Many South Carolinians are descendants of the state's earliest settlers. Some of them still own the same houses and land.

New residents have also been arriving. Small towns are growing in the Blue Ridge Mountains. People from the North have retired along the coast.

European Backgrounds
Almost 70 percent of South Carolinians have European backgrounds. Many of them are English, German, French, or Scotch-Irish.

Some of South Carolina's new residents are people from the North. They came to retire along the coast.

Some South Carolina settlers built huge farms called plantations. Many of them still stand today.

European settlers came to South Carolina to make a living. Many bought land for farming. They raised rice and indigo plants in the Low Country. Indigo plants are used to make blue dye. Some people built huge farms called plantations.

Welsh and German farmers bought land in the Piedmont. French settlers founded the town of Abbeville. Some Scottish settlers traded with Native Americans.

African Americans

About 30 percent of South Carolinians are African American. Most of them descended from West African slaves brought on ships from Africa. Plantation owners and some farmers bought the Africans to work on their farms.

By 1860, slaves made up about 75 percent of South Carolina's population. About 10,000 free African Americans also lived in South Carolina at that time.

After the Civil War, the African slaves were freed. They were made citizens of the United States and were allowed to vote. In the 1890s, South Carolina's government passed segregation laws. Segregation laws were laws that kept African Americans separate from whites. They were forced to go to different schools, restaurants, and parks.

In the early 1900s, thousands of African Americans left South Carolina. They went north to find a better life.

By the 1970s, the federal government required that all public places be open to all people. This is called desegregation. Today, South Carolinians of all races work together and go to school together.

The Gullah-Speaking People

The Gullah (Guh-LAY)-speaking people are African Americans and others that live on South Carolina's Sea Islands. Their ancestors lived and worked on the islands.

These people speak English and the Gullah language. Gullah blends English and West African languages. This language is heard on St. Helena and other islands along the coast.

These African Americans make their living from farming, fishing, and working in factories. Some make baskets from the islands' grasses.

Native Americans

In the 1500s, almost 20,000 Native Americans lived in South Carolina. In the 1800s, white settlers seeking land pushed them from the land onto reservations. Today, only 8,000 live there.

South Carolina has one reservation. A reservation is land set aside for use by Native Americans. The Catawba Reservation is near Rock Hill. The pottery made on the reservation is well known.

Some of the Gullah-speaking people sell baskets made from island grasses.

Other Ethnic Groups

South Carolina also has people from different countries. More than 40,000 Hispanic Americans live in South Carolina. They speak Spanish or have Spanish-speaking backgrounds. Most of them are from Mexico and Puerto Rico. People with Cuban backgrounds have come from Florida.

About 21,000 Asian Americans also live in South Carolina. Their families came from the Philippines, China, Japan, Korea, and Vietnam.

Chapter 4

South Carolina History

The first people entered South Carolina about 10,000 years ago. By the 1500s, about 50 Native American groups lived there. The Cherokee were the largest group.

European Explorers and Settlers

Spanish explorers landed at Winyah Bay in 1521. They started a settlement in 1526. In 1562, French people settled near present-day Beaufort. Neither group lasted long. Many settlers died from disease and hunger.

In the 1600s, the English settled 13 colonies along the Atlantic Ocean. A colony is a group of

Charleston opened the Dock Street Theatre, which was the first theater in the nation.

people who settle in distant lands but remain subject to their native country.

English settlers founded Charles Towne in 1670. This was South Carolina's first permanent European settlement. Now it is known as Charleston.

The English Colony

South Carolina became a rich colony. It was the only one growing rice and indigo. These crops were shipped to England and sold.

Charleston became an important center of trade. Rich planters and merchants built large houses called mansions there. America's first theater and first museum opened there, too.

The Revolutionary War

In the 1760s, England began heavily taxing the 13 colonies. The colonies declared their independence in 1776.

South Carolinians held off the English army until 1780. Then the English captured Charleston.

An important Revolutionary War battle was won at Kings Mountain.

"Face to the Hill!"

That was the cry, before he fell,
of Major William Chronicle, age
25, as he led his small band of
South Fork boys up this end of
the ridge. Soon William Rabb,
Captain John Mattocks and John
Boyd also fell. This monument
memorializes these four men,
friends in life, who died
here together.

Kings Mountain
Battlefield Trail

The first shots of the Civil War were fired on Fort Sumter.

Colonial armies in South Carolina won two important battles. These were at Kings Mountain in 1780 and Cowpens in 1781. The English left Charleston in 1782. The Revolutionary War ended in 1783.

The new nation wrote the U.S. Constitution in 1787. In 1788, South Carolina approved the Constitution. It was the eighth state. Columbia became the state capital.

The Civil War

In the early 1800s, South Carolina became a cotton-growing state. Cotton farmers needed many slaves to harvest this crop.

Many Northerners were against slavery. Abraham Lincoln, a Northerner, was elected president in November 1860. Southerners feared he would outlaw slavery.

South Carolina seceded from the Union in December 1860. To secede means to formally withdraw. Ten other states soon followed. In April 1861, Southern troops fired on Fort Sumter. This was a Union fort in Charleston Harbor. These were the first shots of the Civil War (1861-1865).

South Carolina suffered during the war. Union ships stopped trade at Charleston. Union troops under General William Tecumseh Sherman burned Columbia. They also burned many farms and plantations.

Reconstruction

After the Union won the war, the South underwent Reconstruction. This means South Carolina reorganized and reestablished itself. The African slaves were given their freedom. They

Cotton was the major crop until boll weevils began destroying it. Then, farmers started growing other things.

were also given citizenship and the right to vote by changes to the U.S. Constitution. In 1868, South Carolina had to write a new state constitution.

Other changes also came to South Carolina. Textiles became the state's leading business. Textiles are yarns, fibers, and cloth. Poor farmers no longer able to farm became factory workers. By 1895, African Americans had lost many rights. South Carolina became segregated.

World Wars and the Depression

The United States entered World War I (1914-1918) in 1917. Army training camps opened throughout the state. Charleston had a naval training center.

After the war, beetles called boll weevils ruined many cotton crops. South Carolina farmers started to grow tobacco, soybeans, and fruits. They no longer planted only cotton.

The Great Depression (1929-1939) hurt the whole country. South Carolina mills closed. Workers lost their jobs. Prices for crops fell.

In 1941, the United States entered World War II (1939-1945). The Navy Yard at Charleston built about 200 fighting ships.

Recent Changes

After the war, African Americans began winning back their rights. They voted in federal elections in 1947. By the 1970s, segregation ended.

In the 1960s, northern companies started to move to South Carolina. Since the 1980s, companies from other countries have arrived, too. They have built new factories and textile mills. These new plants employ thousands of South Carolinians. South Carolina is one of the fastest-growing southern states.

Chapter 5

South Carolina Business

Manufacturing is South Carolina's largest business. Service industries come in second. Trade, government, and tourism are major South Carolina service industries. Farming is still important in the state. Fishing and mining are other South Carolina businesses.

Manufacturing

South Carolina is a leading textile-making state. Most textile mills are in the northwest. The mills spin thread and weave cloth.

Companies from other countries have also built plants in the northwest. One of them is a French

Fishing is a major South Carolina industry.

Tourism has grown into a big business. Visitors to the state spend about $6 billion each year.

tire company. A German car company makes BMWs in Greer.

South Carolina makes the most money from its chemicals. Dyes, medicines, and soaps are leading chemical products.

Service Industries

Of the service industries, trade employs the most South Carolinians. Buying and selling goods is important throughout the state.

Many South Carolinians also work for the government. Some work at the Savannah River Nuclear Power Plant. Others teach at state universities and colleges.

Tourism has grown into one of South Carolina's biggest businesses. Visitors to the state spend about $6 billion each year.

Agriculture

Tobacco is the state's leading crop. Soybeans and cotton are also important. Pecans and peanuts grow well, too. Peaches, watermelon, grapes, and strawberries are leading fruits.

Beef cattle and hogs are popular South Carolina livestock. Farmers also raise chickens and turkeys. Thoroughbred horses are raised in west-central South Carolina. They race throughout the country.

Fishing and Mining

Fishing and mining are small businesses in the state. Shrimp, clams, crabs, and oysters are the main catches.

Granite and limestone are the main mining products. Kaolin clay is found in west-central South Carolina. This clay is used to make fine china dishes.

Chapter 6

Seeing the Sights

Visitors have much to see and do in South Carolina. Some visit plantation homes and battlefields. Others hunt, fish, swim, and hike.

The Grand Strand

Myrtle Beach is the best-known town on the Grand Strand. The world's longest sand sculpture was built there in 1991. It was a 86,535-foot-long (25,960-meter-long) building. About 10,000 people helped make it.

To the south is Brookgreen Gardens. It is on the grounds of an old rice plantation. More than 500 sculptures stand there. One is a life-size sculpture of an alligator.

Brookgreen Gardens has more than 500 sculptures.

Charleston

Farther south along the coast stands Charleston. It lies between the Ashley and Cooper rivers.

Charles Towne Landing is on the Ashley River. South Carolina's first English settlement was built there. A copy of the settlers' fort stands there now. Visitors can also see a 1670s ship and garden.

The Old Exchange building stands in downtown Charleston. The Provost Dungeon is in the basement. The English held prisoners there during the Revolutionary War.

The Citadel is across the Ashley River. It is the state's military college. Every Friday afternoon, visitors can watch a parade there. Students march in dress uniforms.

The Sea Islands

South of Charleston are the Sea Islands. St. Helena Island is home to many Gullah-speaking people. Penn Center is there. This school was established during the Civil War for freed slaves. In the 1960s, Dr. Martin Luther

King Jr. and other civil rights leaders held meetings there.

Farther south is Hilton Head Island. Cotton plantations once covered the island. Now it has golf courses, tennis courts, and huge resorts.

Central South Carolina

Fields of tobacco grow in the northeast. Lake City and Mullins have the state's biggest tobacco auctions.

The Browntown Museum is east of Lake City. It is a farm from the 1830s. Museum visitors can see the farmhouse, outhouse, and cotton gin. They can learn about daily life before the Civil War.

Columbia is in the middle of the state. The State House is the capitol building. Its walls still have shell marks from Union guns fired during the Civil War.

Columbia is also home to the University of South Carolina. The school's mascot is a gamecock. About 25,000 students attend the university. They enjoy watching the Gamecock football and basketball teams.

Northwestern South Carolina

Rock Hill is in northern South Carolina. Farther north of this city is Carowinds. This amusement park sits along the North Carolina border. Park visitors sometimes become part of movie and television scenes. The park includes roller coasters and water rides.

Farther west are two Revolutionary War battlefields. Visitors can walk through Kings Mountain National Military Park. Cowpens National Battlefield also has a walking trail.

The Blue Ridge

Greer is southwest of Cowpens. BMW Zentrum is there. This museum shows BMW vehicles and engines.

The Cherokee Foothills Scenic Highway starts southeast of Cowpens. It passes through the Blue Ridge Mountains. Drivers enjoy the small towns along the highway.

The Chattanooga River rushes along South Carolina's northwestern border. Kayakers tumble through its rapids. The river flows through the Sumter National Forest. The forest has hiking trails and campsites.

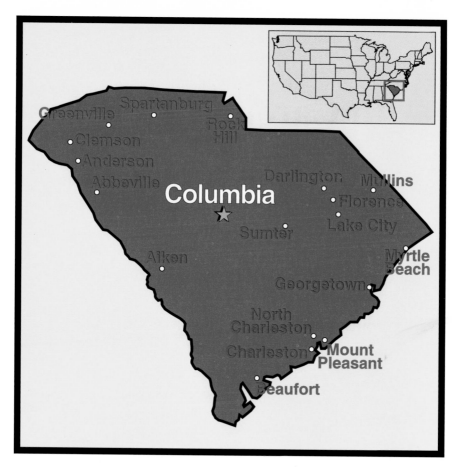

Clemson is between Greer and the
Chattanooga River. It is the home of Clemson
University. About 17,000 students go there.

Fort Hill is on the school's grounds. Fort
Hill was the home of John C. Calhoun. He was
vice president of the United States from 1825
to 1832. The home has furniture once owned
by the Calhoun family.

South Carolina Time Line

10,000 B.C.—The first people reach South Carolina.

A.D. 1526—The Spanish start the first European settlement in South Carolina.

1670—English settlers establish Charles Town, South Carolina's first permanent European settlement.

1729—South Carolina becomes a colony of England.

1736—The nation's first theater, the Dock Street Theatre, opens in Charleston.

1786—Columbia becomes the new capital of South Carolina.

1788—South Carolina becomes the eighth state.

1830—The first steam locomotive in the United States begins service in South Carolina.

1860—South Carolina becomes the first state to leave the Union.

1861—Confederate troops fire on Fort Sumter, starting the Civil War.

1865—Union troops cause much damage in South Carolina; the Civil War ends.

1868—South Carolina is readmitted to the Union.

1895—South Carolina adopts a new constitution that limits the rights of African Americans.

1953—The Savannah River Nuclear Energy Plant opens near Aiken.

1963—The first African-American student enrolls at Clemson University.

1971—Desegregation of South Carolina's public places is completed.

1989—Hurricane Hugo kills about 20 South Carolinians and causes about $5 billion in damages.

1995—The U.S. government closes the Charleston naval base; a U.S. court rules that the Citadel must admit women.

1995-1996—Suspected racially based arson destroys several African-American churches throughout the state.

Famous
South Carolinians

Sara Ayers (1919-) Potter who uses Indian traditions in her works; born on the Catawba Indian Reservation near Rock Hill.

Cardinal Joseph Louis Bernardin (1928-1996) Catholic priest who became Archbishop of Chicago; born in Columbia.

Mark Clark (1896-1984) U.S. Army general who led Allied forces in Europe during World War II; president of the Citadel (1954-1966).

Joe Frazier (1944-) Championship heavyweight boxer (1970-1973); born in Beaufort.

Althea Gibson (1927-) First African-American woman to win the Wimbledon and U.S. National tennis championships; born in Silver.

Dizzy Gillespie (1917-1993) Trumpet player and composer who helped create the bebop jazz style of the 1940s; born in Cheraw.

Jesse Jackson (1941-) Minister and civil rights leader; born in Greenville.

Eartha Kitt (1928-) Singer, dancer, and actress; played Catwoman on television's *Batman*; born in North.

Francis Marion (1732-1795) Military leader during the Revolutionary War who used his knowledge of South Carolina's swamps to fight the British; nicknamed the "Swamp Fox"; born in Winyah.

Ronald McNair (1950-1986) Astronaut who was the second African American to travel in space; killed on board the space shuttle Challenger when it exploded; grew up in Lake City.

Robert Mills (1781-1855) Architect who designed the Washington Monument in Washington, D.C.; born in Charleston.

Eliza Lucas Pinckney (1722-1793) Started the indigo industry in South Carolina.

Strom Thurmond (1902-) Governor of South Carolina (1947-1951) and U.S. senator (1955-present); born in Edgefield.

Vanna White (1957-) Television personality famous for turning letters on *Wheel of Fortune*; born in Conway.

Words to Know

boll weevil—a beetle that destroys cotton seeds and fiber

colony—a group of people who settle distant lands but remain governed by their native country

desegregate—to make schools, parks, restaurants, and other public places available to people of all races

humid—air that is heavy with moisture

hurricane—a strong windstorm that forms over the ocean and causes great damage when it reaches land

indigo—a plant that can be made into a blue dye for clothing

mansion—a large house

plantation—a large farm that usually grows one main crop

reservation—land set aside for use by Native Americans

secede—to break away from a country or organization

segregate—to keep people of different races apart

textile—yarns, fibers, or cloth

tourism—the business of providing services such as food and lodging for travelers

To Learn More

Aylesworth, Thomas G. and Virginia L. Aylesworth. *Lower Atlantic*. Let's Discover the States. New York: Chelsea House, 1988.

Fradin, Dennis Brindell. *South Carolina*. Sea to Shining Sea. Chicago: Children's Press, 1992.

Kent, Deborah. *South Carolina*. America the Beautiful. Chicago: Children's Press, 1990.

Krull, Kathleen. *Bridges to Change: How Kids Live on a South Carolina Sea Island*. New York: Lodestar Books, 1995.

Useful Addresses

BMW Zentrum
1400 Highway 101 South
Greer, SC 29659

Joe Weatherly NMPA Stock Car Hall of Fame
1301 Harry Byrd Highway
Darlington, SC 29532

Old Powder Magazine
79 Cumberland
Charleston, SC 29423

South Carolina Cotton Museum
115 North Main Street
Bishopville, SC 29010

South Carolina Criminal Justice Hall of Fame
5400 Broad River Road
Columbia, SC 29202

Thoroughbred Hall of Fame
Hopeland Gardens
Whiskey Road
Aiken, SC 29801

Internet Sites

City.Net South Carolina
http://www.city.net/countries/united_states/
south_carolina/

Travel.org South Carolina
http://travel.org/s-carol.html

State of South Carolina
http://www.state.sc.us/

Darlington Raceway
http://www.nascar.com/tracks/darlingt.html

Index